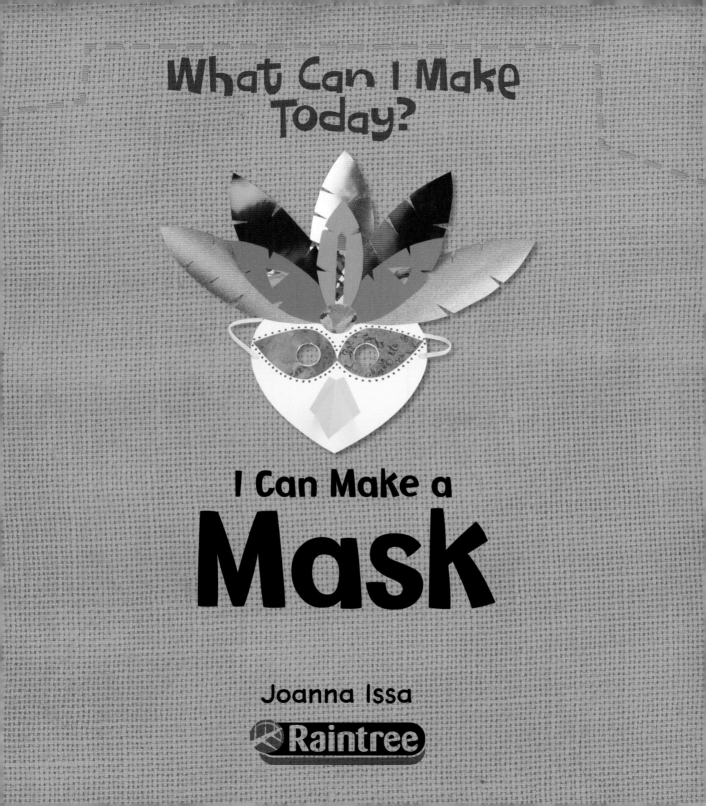

What Can I Make Today?

I Can Make a
Mask

Joanna Issa

Raintree

Raintree is an imprint of Capstone Global Library Limited, a company incorporated in England and Wales having its registered office at 7 Pilgrim Street, London, EC4V 6LB – Registered company number: 6695582

Edited by Penny West
Designed by Philippa Jenkins
Picture research by Elizabeth Alexander
Originated by Capstone Global Library Ltd
Production by Victoria Fitzgerald
Printed and bound in China

ISBN 978 1 406 28404 1
18 17 16 15 14
10 9 8 7 6 5 4 3 2 1

British Library Cataloguing in Publication Data
A full catalogue record for this book is available from the British Library.

Acknowledgements
We would like to thank Capstone Publishers/ © Karon Dubke for permission to reproduce photographs.

Cover photograph reproduced with permission of Capstone Publishers/ © Karon Dubke.

We would like to thank Philippa Jenkins and Elizabeth Alexander for their invaluable help in the preparation of this book.

Every effort has been made to contact copyright holders of material reproduced in this book. Any omissions will be rectified in subsequent printings if notice is given to the publishers.

Contents

Some words are shown in bold, like this. You can find them in the glossary on page 23.

What do I need to make a mask?

To make the bird mask, you will need the head, beak and eye templates, card, paper, a pencil, scissors, sticky tape, a **split pin** and **elastic**.

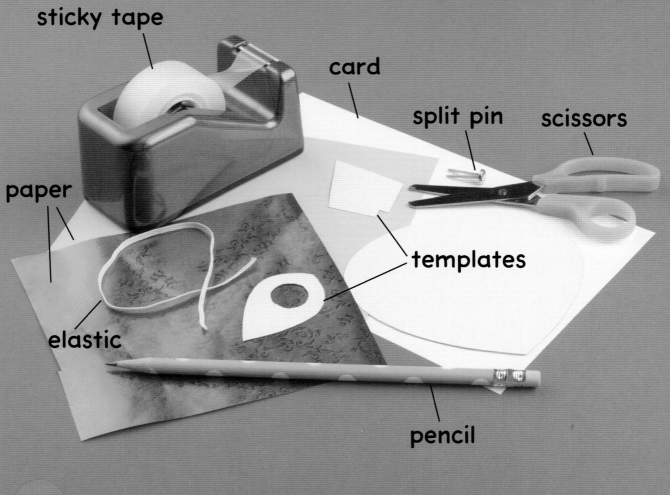

sticky tape

card

split pin

scissors

paper

templates

elastic

pencil

To make the templates, photocopy pages 21 and 22 and then cut out each shape.

paper

foil

templates

glue

glitter

pen

To make the feathers, you will need the feather templates, paper, **foil**, a pen, glitter and glue.

Make the head

Put the head template on the card and draw around it. Then cut out the head.

Make the eyes

Put the eye template on some paper and draw around it twice to make two eyes.

Ask an adult to help you draw eyeholes on the eye shapes and the head. Then cut them out.

Ask for adult help

8

Make the beak

Put the beak template on some paper and draw around it. Cut out the beak. Fold it down the middle to make a pointy end.

Make the feathers

Put the big feather template on some paper or **foil**. Draw around it six times to make six feathers.

Put the small feather template on some paper or foil. Draw around it three times to make three feathers. Cut out your feathers.

Cut out shapes from colourful paper and **foil** to **decorate** your feathers.

You could also paint them or add glitter.

Decorate the mask

Glue the feathers, eyes and the beak onto your mask.

Make a line of dots around the eyes
with a pen or with glitter.

Make two holes in the sides of the mask with a **split pin**. Push **elastic** through the holes and fix with tape.

Make an owl mask

Use the templates on pages 21 and 22 to make a different mask. Draw around the head template as before. Cut it out.

You can add large eyes to make an owl mask.

You can add different coloured feathers and a small beak.

What can you make today?

You could make a colourful bird mask for a party or for dressing up.

Mask templates

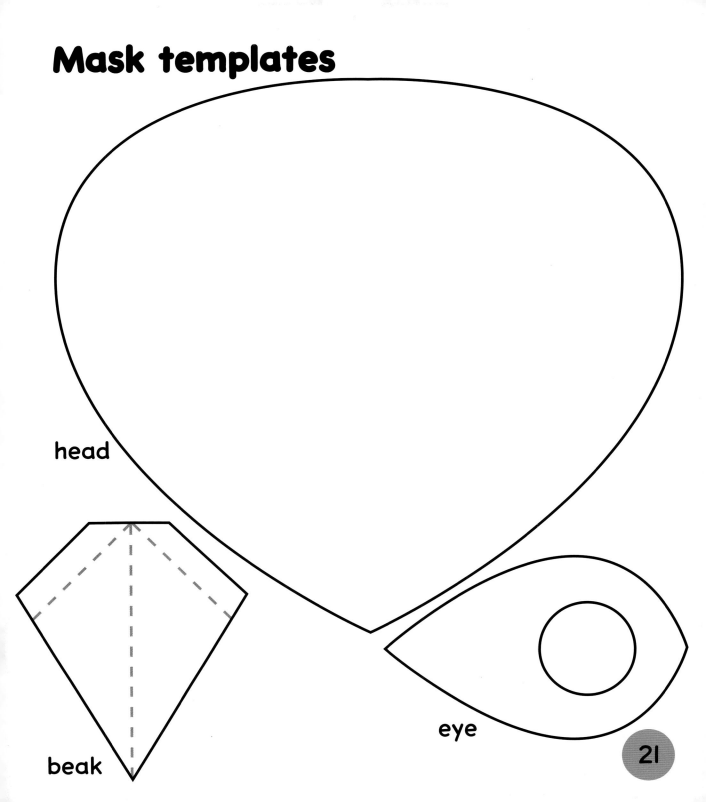

head

beak

eye

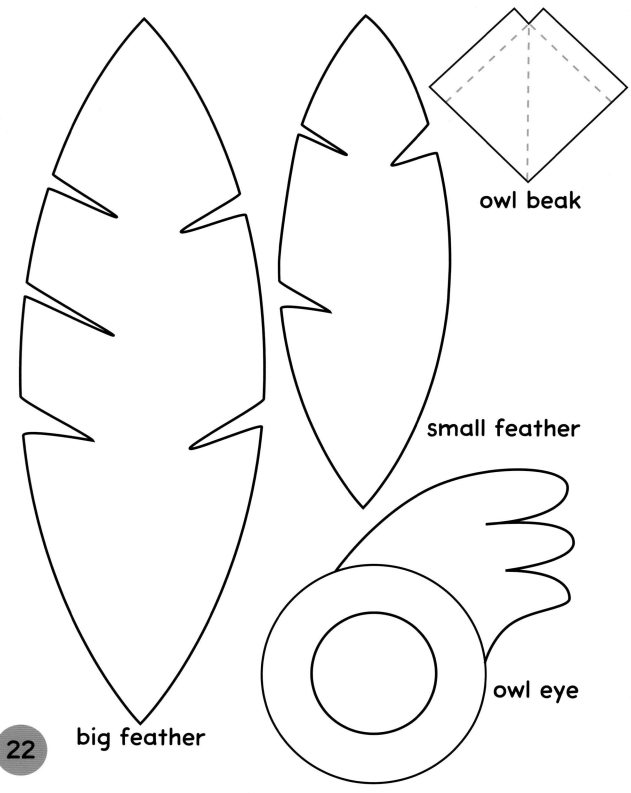

owl beak

small feather

owl eye

big feather

22

Picture glossary

decorate add colour or objects to make something interesting

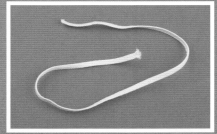

elastic thin fabric or cord that can be stretched

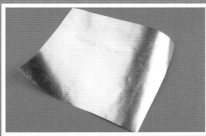

foil very thin metal sheets

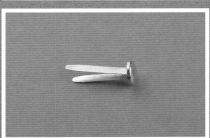

split pin metal pin with ends that bend

Find out more

Books

365 Things to do with Paper and Cardboard (Usborne Activities), Fiona Watt (Usborne, 2011)

Masks (World of Design), Ruth Thomson (Franklin Watts, 2011)

Masks and Face Painting (Start with Art), Isabel Thomas (Raintree, 2011)

Websites

www.enchantedlearning.com/crafts
Visit the Enchanted Learning website to find craft projects using everyday household materials.

www.prm.ox.ac.uk/family-athome.html
On this website, you can read about fun projects to do at home, including festival masks.

Index

24